500 SPACE FACTS FOR KIDS

First Published in 2023 by Squid Press.

All rights reserved. This book is not to be reproduced, transmitted or stored in any information retrieval system in any form or by any means without the prior consent.

This cover and interior has been designed using assets from Macrovector on Freepik.com.

Disclaimer Notice: All names, characters, trademarks and trade names within this book are the property of the respective owners. This is a book published and has not been licensed, approved, sponsored or endorsed by any person or entity.

This book is accurate as of March 2023.

OUR UNIVERSE

The universe is estimated to be around 13.8 billion years old.

The universe is believed to have begun with a big bang, a massive explosion that occurred around 13.8 billion years ago. The Big Bang theory was first proposed by a Belgian astronomer named Georges Lemaître in 1927.

Before the Big Bang, the universe was a single, infinitely hot and dense point.

The first atoms formed about 380,000 years after the Big Bang.

The first stars and galaxies formed about 200 million years after the Big Bang.

The cosmic microwave background radiation is the afterglow of the Big Bang, and it can be detected throughout the universe.

Some scientists believe that the Big Bang was not a one-time event, but rather one of many cycles of expansion and contraction in a never-ending cosmic cycle.

The universe is constantly expanding, meaning that the distances between galaxies and other objects in space are getting larger over time.

There are at least 100 billion galaxies in the observable universe.

The Milky Way is the galaxy that contains our solar system, and it is estimated to contain at least 100 billion stars.

The universe is filled with invisible dark matter, which scientists believe makes up about 85% of all matter in the universe.

The universe is also filled with dark energy, a mysterious force that is causing the expansion of the universe to accelerate.

The fastest known object in the universe is a stream of particles called cosmic rays, which can travel at speeds up to 99.9999999999999999999951% of the speed of light.

The universe contains countless planets and other celestial bodies, many of which may harbor life.

The largest known structure in the universe is a collection of galaxies known as the Hercules-Corona Borealis Great Wall, which is estimated to be around 10 billion light-years across.

The smallest known particle in the universe is the quark, which makes up protons and neutrons.

The universe is full of radiation, including cosmic rays, gamma rays, and other types of high-energy particles.

Black holes are areas of space where the gravitational pull is so strong that nothing can escape, not even light.

Supernovas are some of the most spectacular events in the universe, occurring when a star explodes and releases a burst of energy that can briefly outshine an entire galaxy. Gamma-ray bursts are even more energetic, releasing beams of high-energy radiation that can be detected from billions of light-years away.

Neutron stars and pulsars are some of the most fascinating objects in the universe. Neutron stars are incredibly dense and have the mass of about 1.4 suns packed into an area the size of a city, while pulsars emit beams of radiation that can be detected from Earth.

Scientists use telescopes and other instruments to study the universe and learn more about its properties and characteristics.

The study of the universe is known as astronomy.

The oldest known object in the universe is a star known as SMSS J031300.36-670839.3, which is estimated to be around 13.8 billion years old.

The universe is filled with cosmic dust, tiny particles of matter that float through space.

The universe contains vast clouds of gas and dust that can eventually collapse to form stars and planets.

The largest known planet in the universe is WASP-17b, which is around twice the size of Jupiter.

The universe contains countless asteroids and comets, many of which have collided with Earth throughout its history.

Scientists continue to study the universe and make new discoveries, revealing more about its vastness, complexity, and beauty.

The universe is estimated to contain around 10 billion trillion trillion stars, which is a number so large it's almost impossible to imagine!

The universe is thought to be flat, meaning that it has no curvature, based on the latest measurements from scientific instruments.

There are several theories about how the universe will end, including the Big Freeze, the Big Crunch, and the Big Rip.

The universe contains dark matter, a substance that cannot be seen but which scientists know is there because of its gravitational effects on visible matter.

The universe also contains dark energy, a mysterious force that is causing the expansion of the universe to accelerate.

The oldest known star in the universe is a star known as SM0313-6708, which is thought to be around 13.6 billion years old.

The universe is filled with cosmic rays, which are high-energy particles that come from outside our solar system.

The most massive known star in the universe is R136a1, which is estimated to have a mass of around 315 times that of our sun.

The universe is home to a wide variety of galaxies, including spiral galaxies, elliptical galaxies, and irregular galaxies.

The largest known galaxy in the universe is IC 1101, which is estimated to be around 6 million light-years across.

The universe is believed to be home to a large number of black holes, which are regions of space where the gravitational pull is so strong that not even light can escape.

The universe also contains supermassive black holes, which are found at the centers of most galaxies and can have masses of millions or even billions of suns.

The universe contains numerous nebulae, which are clouds of gas and dust that can be hundreds of light-years across.

The Crab Nebula, located in the constellation Taurus, is one of the most famous nebulae in the universe, and was created by the explosion of a supernova in the year 1054.

The universe is home to a variety of exoplanets, which are planets outside our solar system that orbit other stars.

The universe is filled with cosmic microwave background radiation, which is leftover radiation from the Big Bang and can be detected by sensitive scientific instruments.

The universe is also home to a vast network of cosmic filaments and voids, which make up the structure of the universe at the largest scales.

The universe contains countless galaxies and other objects that emit powerful jets of energy, such as quasars and blazars.

The most distant object in the universe ever observed is a galaxy known as GN-z11, which is estimated to be around 13.4 billion years old and located 32 billion light-years away.

The universe contains numerous types of particles, including photons, neutrinos, and dark matter particles.

The universe is constantly changing, with stars being born and dying, galaxies merging and colliding, and the expansion of the universe continuing to accelerate.

Scientists are still working to unravel many of the mysteries of the universe, including the nature of dark matter and dark energy.

The universe is full of beautiful and awe-inspiring phenomena, such as the Northern and Southern Lights, or auroras, which are caused by charged particles from the sun interacting with Earth's magnetic field.

Despite our current understanding of the universe, there is still much to learn and explore, and new discoveries are being made all the time by scientists and astronomers

Scientists have recently discovered a new type of celestial object called "blanets", which are objects that are bigger than a planet but smaller than a star, and emit very little light.

The universe is expanding faster than scientists previously thought, which means that it's getting bigger at an even faster rate than previously estimated.

If you could travel at the speed of light, it would take you over 4 years to reach the nearest star to our solar system, Proxima Centauri.

THE SOLAR SYSTEM

The Milky Way's nearest neighbor galaxy is the Andromeda Galaxy, which is about 2.5 million light-years away.

The Milky Way is part of a group of galaxies called the Local Group, which also includes the Andromeda Galaxy and several smaller galaxies.

The Milky Way has a magnetic field, which is responsible for the beautiful aurora borealis and aurora australis that can be seen in the Earth's polar regions.

The Milky Way is named after the band of milky-white light that can be seen across the sky at night, which is caused by the combined light of billions of stars.

The Milky Way is not static, and it is constantly interacting with other galaxies and absorbing smaller galaxies.

The Milky Way has been around for about 13.6 billion years, which is roughly the same age as the universe itself.

The universe is so big that if you tried to count all the stars in the Milky Way galaxy at a rate of one per second, it would take you over 2,000 years!

The Milky Way's stars are not evenly distributed, and they are clustered together in regions called globular clusters.

The Milky Way's shape is constantly changing, and it is believed to have undergone several mergers and collisions with other galaxies throughout its history.

The Milky Way is a fascinating object to study, and scientists continue to learn new things about it every day through observations and research.

Mercury is the smallest planet in our solar system. It is even smaller than some moons in the solar system!

Mercury is named after the Roman messenger god, Mercury. In Roman mythology, Mercury was the god of commerce, communication, and travel.

Mercury is the closest planet to the Sun, so it gets really hot! During the day, temperatures can reach up to 800 degrees Fahrenheit (430 degrees Celsius), but at night they can drop to minus 290 degrees Fahrenheit (-180 degrees Celsius).

Mercury has a rocky surface that is covered in craters, mountains, and valleys. It is very similar to Earth's moon in appearance.

Because Mercury is so close to the Sun, its year is only 88 Earth days long! That means it takes Mercury just 88 days to orbit around the Sun.

Despite its small size, Mercury is the second densest planet in our solar system, after Earth. That means it has a lot of mass packed into a small space.

Mercury doesn't have any moons or rings like some of the other planets in our solar system.

Mercury is one of the five planets that you can see from Earth with just your eyes. It is usually visible just before sunrise or just after sunset.

Because Mercury is so close to the Sun, it has been visited by only two spacecraft: NASA's Mariner 10 in the 1970s and Messenger in the 2000s.

Mercury has a very thin atmosphere that is made up of mostly helium and hydrogen. Because of its weak gravity, the atmosphere is constantly being blown away by the solar wind from the Sun.

Venus is the second planet from the Sun and is often called Earth's sister planet because they are similar in size.

Venus is named after the Roman goddess of love and beauty. In Roman mythology, Venus was the goddess of love, beauty, and fertility.

Venus is the hottest planet in our solar system. Its surface temperature can reach up to 864 degrees Fahrenheit (462 degrees Celsius) - hot enough to melt lead!

Venus has a thick atmosphere made mostly of carbon dioxide, which causes a greenhouse effect and makes it even hotter.

Venus has no moons or rings, unlike some of the other planets in our solar system.

Venus rotates in the opposite direction of most planets in our solar system, meaning that its day is longer than its year!

Venus is the brightest planet in our solar system and can often be seen in the night sky just after sunset or just before sunrise.

Venus has many volcanoes and lava plains on its surface, suggesting that it is geologically active.

The surface of Venus is very dry and rocky, with many craters and mountain ranges.

Because of its similarity to Earth in size and composition, scientists are interested in studying Venus to learn more about how planets form and evolve over time.

The Earth is the third planet from the Sun and is the only planet known to support life.

The Earth is approximately 4.5 billion years old and is constantly changing and evolving.

The Earth's surface is covered by about 71% water, making it a "blue planet."

The Earth has a diameter of approximately 12,742 kilometers (7,918 miles) and is the fifth-largest planet in the solar system.

The Earth's atmosphere is made up of several layers, including the troposphere, stratosphere, mesosphere, thermosphere, and exosphere.

The Earth rotates on its axis once every 24 hours, causing day and night.

The Earth orbits around the Sun once every 365.25 days, which is the length of a year.

The Earth's magnetic field helps protect it from harmful solar radiation and charged particles.

The Earth has one natural satellite, the Moon, which orbits around it once every 27.3 days.

The Earth's highest point is Mount Everest, which stands at 8,848 meters (29,029 feet) above sea level.

The Earth's lowest point is the Challenger Deep, which is located in the Mariana Trench and is approximately 11 kilometers (7 miles) below sea level.

The Earth experiences four seasons (spring, summer, fall, and winter) due to its tilt on its axis.

The Earth has a rich diversity of life, including plants, animals, and microorganisms.

The Earth's oceans are home to many fascinating creatures, including whales, dolphins, sharks, and sea turtles.

The Earth's climate is affected by many factors, including greenhouse gases, solar radiation, and ocean currents.

The Earth has a rich geological history, and its rocks and fossils provide clues about its past.

The Earth's atmosphere is composed of several gases, including nitrogen, oxygen, carbon dioxide, and trace amounts of other gases.

The Earth's ozone layer helps protect it from harmful ultraviolet radiation from the Sun.

The Earth is constantly changing due to processes such as erosion, plate tectonics, and volcanic activity.

The Earth is a beautiful and fascinating planet, and it is our responsibility to protect and care for it for future generations.

Our moon is the fifth largest moon in our solar system.

The surface area of the moon is about 14.6 million square miles.

The moon is the closest celestial body to Earth, at an average distance of about 238,855 miles.

The moon is about one quarter the size of Earth.

The moon is believed to have formed about 4.5 billion years ago.

The moon has no atmosphere, which means there is no weather or wind on the moon.

The temperature on the moon can vary from -280°F to 260°F.

The moon's gravity is about one-sixth of Earth's gravity.

The moon's surface is covered in craters, mountains, and plains.

The first person to step on the moon was Neil Armstrong in 1969.

The moon's craters are caused by meteoroids and asteroids hitting the surface.

The moon is slowly moving away from Earth at a rate of about 1.5 inches per year.

The moon has no magnetic field, which means it has no protection from solar winds.

The moon's largest crater is called the South Pole-Aitken basin, which is about 1,550 miles in diameter.

The moon's phases were first recorded by ancient civilizations, including the Greeks and the Chinese.

The moon is the only natural satellite of Earth.

The moon is not a light source, but reflects sunlight.

The moon's orbit is slightly tilted, which causes it to appear differently in different parts of the world.

The moon has a very weak and irregular magnetic field.

The moon's surface is constantly bombarded by micrometeoroids and cosmic rays.

Mars is often called the Red Planet because it appears as a reddish color in the night sky.

Mars is named after the Roman god of war. In Roman mythology, Mars was the god of war, second in importance only to Jupiter.

Mars is the fourth planet from the Sun and is known for its dusty, rocky terrain and extreme weather patterns.

Mars has the largest volcano in our solar system, called Olympus Mons. It is about three times taller than Mount Everest!

Mars is home to the largest canyon in our solar system, called Valles Marineris. It is about 4,000 kilometers long and up to 7 kilometers deep.

Mars has a very thin atmosphere that is made up mostly of carbon dioxide. The atmospheric pressure on Mars is less than 1% of Earth's atmospheric pressure.

Mars has two small moons, Phobos and Deimos, which are irregularly shaped and thought to be asteroids that were captured by Mars' gravity.

Mars has seasons, just like Earth. This is because Mars' axis is tilted in a similar way to Earth's axis.

Scientists believe that Mars may have had liquid water on its surface in the past, which could mean that it had the right conditions for life to exist.

NASA and other space agencies have sent several spacecraft to Mars to study its surface, atmosphere, and geology. The most recent mission is NASA's Perseverance rover, which landed on Mars in February 2021 and is currently exploring the planet's surface.

Jupiter is the largest planet in our solar system. It is so big that you could fit all the other planets in the solar system inside it!

Jupiter is named after the king of the Roman gods. In Roman mythology, Jupiter was the god of the sky and thunder.

Jupiter has a really strong magnetic field. It is about 20,000 times stronger than Earth's magnetic field.

Jupiter has at least 79 moons! Some of the most famous ones are Io, Europa, Ganymede, and Callisto.

One of Jupiter's moons, Io, is the most volcanically active place in the solar system. It has more than 400 active volcanoes!

Jupiter's Great Red Spot is a giant storm that has been raging for more than 300 years. It is so big that you could fit two Earths inside it.

Because Jupiter is made mostly of gas, it doesn't have a solid surface like Earth. If you were to try to land on Jupiter, you would just sink down into its atmosphere.

Jupiter is known for its colorful bands of clouds. The different colors come from the different chemicals that make up the clouds.

Jupiter's day is only about 10 hours long! That means that one day on Jupiter is shorter than one day on Earth.

Jupiter is one of the five planets that you can see from Earth with just your eyes, and it is usually one of the brightest objects in the night sky.

Saturn is the sixth planet from the Sun and is known for its beautiful rings, which are made up of ice particles and rocky debris.

Saturn is named after the Roman god of agriculture and harvest. In Roman mythology, Saturn was also known as the god of time.

Saturn is the second-largest planet in our solar system, after Jupiter. It is about nine times wider than Earth.

Saturn has at least 82 moons, the most of any planet in our solar system. Some of its largest moons include Titan, Enceladus, and Mimas.

Saturn's rings are divided into several smaller rings, each with its own unique characteristics and properties.

Saturn has a very fast rotation rate, which means that its day is only about 10.5 Earth hours long.

Saturn has a very low density, which means that if you could find a big enough bathtub, Saturn would float in it!

Saturn's atmosphere is mostly made up of hydrogen and helium, with small amounts of other gases like methane and ammonia.

Saturn's largest moon, Titan, is the only moon in our solar system with a thick atmosphere. It is so thick that it hides the surface from view.

NASA's Cassini spacecraft orbited Saturn from 2004 to 2017, studying its rings, moons, and atmosphere. Cassini also landed a probe on Saturn's moon, Titan, and discovered lakes of liquid methane on its surface.

Uranus is the seventh planet from the Sun and is known for its distinct blue-green color.

Uranus is named after the Greek god of the sky. In Greek mythology, Uranus was the father of the Titans and the grandfather of Zeus.

Uranus is one of the four gas giant planets in our solar system, along with Jupiter, Saturn, and Neptune.

Uranus has a unique orientation in our solar system - its axis is tilted at an angle of 98 degrees, which means that its poles are almost in the plane of its orbit.

Because of its extreme tilt, Uranus has very long seasons. Each season lasts about 20 Earth years.

Uranus has at least 27 known moons, all of which are named after characters in the works of William Shakespeare and Alexander Pope.

Uranus has a faint ring system made up of millions of small particles. The rings were discovered in 1977 by scientists studying the planet from Earth.

Uranus is one of the coldest planets in our solar system, with temperatures that can reach as low as -224 degrees Celsius (-371 degrees Fahrenheit).

Uranus has a thin atmosphere made up mostly of hydrogen, helium, and methane. The methane in Uranus' atmosphere is what gives it its blue-green color.

Uranus has been visited by only one spacecraft - NASA's Voyager 2 in 1986. Voyager 2 discovered 10 new moons and two new rings around Uranus during its flyby.

Neptune is the eighth planet from the Sun and is known for its beautiful blue color.

Neptune is named after the Roman god of the sea. In Roman mythology, Neptune was the brother of Jupiter and Pluto.

Neptune is one of the four gas giant planets in our solar system, along with Jupiter, Saturn, and Uranus.

Neptune is the farthest planet from the Sun and has a very cold and windy atmosphere.

Neptune has at least 14 known moons, the largest of which is Triton. Triton is the only large moon in our solar system that orbits its planet in a direction opposite to the planet's rotation.

Neptune's atmosphere is made up mostly of hydrogen, helium, and methane. The methane in Neptune's atmosphere is what gives it its blue color.

Neptune has the strongest winds in our solar system, with gusts that can reach up to 2,000 kilometers per hour (1,200 miles per hour).

Neptune has a faint ring system made up of small particles. The rings were discovered in 1989 by scientists studying the planet from Earth.

Neptune has a very active and dynamic atmosphere, with large storms and vortices that can last for years.

NASA's Voyager 2 spacecraft is the only spacecraft to have visited Neptune. Voyager 2 flew past Neptune in 1989, discovering new moons and rings and studying the planet's atmosphere and magnetosphere.

Pluto used to be classified as the ninth planet in our solar system, but in 2006 it was reclassified as a dwarf planet.

Pluto is named after the Roman god of the underworld. In Roman mythology, Pluto was also known as the god of wealth.

Pluto is very small compared to the other planets in our solar system. It is only about one-sixth the size of Earth.

Pluto is located in the Kuiper Belt, a region of our solar system beyond Neptune that is filled with icy objects.

Pluto has five known moons, the largest of which is Charon. Charon is so big compared to Pluto that some scientists consider them to be a binary system.

Pluto has a very thin atmosphere made up mostly of nitrogen, methane, and carbon monoxide. Its atmosphere freezes onto the surface as Pluto moves farther from the Sun in its orbit.

Pluto is very cold, with temperatures that can drop as low as -240 degrees Celsius (-400 degrees Fahrenheit).

Pluto has a reddish-brown color caused by tholins, complex molecules formed from methane and nitrogen in Pluto's atmosphere.

Pluto has a very elliptical orbit that takes it closer to the Sun than Neptune for part of its orbit. This means that sometimes it is actually closer to the Sun than Neptune is.

NASA's New Horizons spacecraft is the only spacecraft to have visited Pluto. New Horizons flew past Pluto in 2015, sending back amazing images and data about the dwarf planet and its moons.

The Sun is a star, a huge ball of hot gas that produces light and heat.

The Sun is located at the center of our solar system, and all of the planets orbit around it.

The Sun is about 4.6 billion years old and is expected to continue shining for another 5 billion years.

The Sun is the largest object in our solar system, with a diameter of about 1.4 million kilometers (865,000 miles).

The Sun is so big that it makes up about 99.86% of the total mass of our solar system.

The surface of the Sun is called the photosphere, and it has a temperature of about 5,500 degrees Celsius (9,932 degrees Fahrenheit).

The Sun's atmosphere has two layers: the chromosphere and the corona. The corona is the outermost layer and is visible during a total solar eclipse.

The Sun's magnetic field is responsible for creating sunspots, which are cooler areas on the surface of the Sun.

The Sun's magnetic field also causes solar flares and coronal mass ejections, which can cause geomagnetic storms on Earth.

The Sun is the ultimate source of energy for all life on Earth. It provides the light and heat necessary for photosynthesis, which is the process that plants use to produce food.

The Sun's energy is also used to generate electricity through solar panels.

The Sun's gravity is so strong that it keeps all of the planets in our solar system in orbit around it.

The Sun rotates on its axis once every 27.3 Earth days.

The Sun is a yellow dwarf star, which means it is relatively small and not as hot as some other stars in the universe.

The Sun's size and temperature are just right to allow life to exist on Earth.

The Sun's energy is created through a process called nuclear fusion, in which hydrogen atoms are fused together to form helium.

The Sun emits light in all colors of the rainbow, but our eyes only see a small portion of this light as visible light.

The Sun has a strong influence on Earth's weather and climate. Changes in the Sun's energy output can affect our planet's temperature and weather patterns.

The Sun's energy output goes through cycles that last about 11 years, during which the number of sunspots and solar flares increases and decreases.

The Sun is not actually yellow - it only appears that way because of the Earth's atmosphere.

The Sun's energy output varies over time, in a cycle that lasts about 11 years.

If you were to stand on the surface of the sun (which is impossible, because it's too hot and would vaporize you instantly), you would weigh about 28 times more than you do on Earth.

The Sun is actually a pretty noisy place – it constantly emits sound waves that can be heard by certain instruments.

Sunlight takes about 8 minutes to reach Earth, traveling at a speed of about 299,792,458 meters per second.

The Sun emits more energy in one second than the entire human race has used in all of history.

SPACE TRAVEL & EXPLORATION

The first animal to travel to space was a dog named Laika, sent by the Soviet Union in 1957.

The first person to orbit the Earth was Yuri Gagarin, a Soviet cosmonaut, in 1961.

The first American to orbit the Earth was John Glenn in 1962.

The first spacecraft to land on the moon was the Soviet Union's Luna 9 in 1966.

The first human to walk on the moon was Neil Armstrong during the Apollo 11 mission in 1969.

The first space station was launched by the Soviet Union in 1971.

The first woman to travel to space was Valentina Tereshkova, a Soviet cosmonaut, in 1963.

The first American woman to travel to space was Sally Ride in 1983.

The Hubble Space Telescope, launched in 1990, has helped scientists study the universe and make many important discoveries.

The International Space Station is a joint project between the United States, Russia, Canada, Europe, and Japan, and has been continuously occupied by humans since 2000.

NASA's Curiosity Rover, which landed on Mars in 2012, has sent back valuable data and images from the planet's surface.

NASA's Parker Solar Probe, launched in 2018, is the fastest spacecraft ever built, reaching speeds of up to 430,000 miles per hour as it studies the sun.

Space exploration has led to many important inventions, such as GPS technology and memory foam.

Astronauts need to exercise regularly to maintain their muscle and bone strength in the microgravity environment of space.

Space food is specially designed to be lightweight, easy to eat, and not crumbly, since crumbs can float around and damage equipment.

The longest single space mission was by Valeri Polyakov, who spent 437 days aboard the Russian space station Mir in 1994-1995.

Space junk, which includes abandoned satellites and other debris, is becoming an increasing problem as more objects are launched into space.

The first private company to launch people into space was SpaceX, founded by Elon Musk, in 2020.

NASA is planning a manned mission to Mars in the 2030s, which would be the first time humans have traveled to another planet.

The first privately-funded mission to the moon was in 2019, when Israeli company SpaceIL launched the Beresheet spacecraft.

NASA's Perseverance Rover, which landed on Mars in 2021, is searching for signs of ancient microbial life on the planet.

In 2021, the Chinese spacecraft Tianwen-1 successfully landed a rover on Mars, becoming the second country to do so.

The largest planet in our solar system is Jupiter, which is more than twice the size of all the other planets combined.

NASA's Voyager 1 spacecraft, launched in 1977, is now the farthest human-made object from Earth and has left our solar system.

The first person to complete a spacewalk was Soviet cosmonaut Alexei Leonov in 1965.

Spacecraft use rockets to escape Earth's gravity and reach space, but then rely on other propulsion methods, such as ion engines, to continue their journey.

The Cassini spacecraft, which explored Saturn and its moons from 2004 to 2017, discovered geysers on the moon Enceladus that could potentially contain signs of life.

The first image of a black hole, located in the center of the Messier 87 galaxy, was captured by the Event Horizon Telescope in 2019.

The first all-civilian mission to space, SpaceX's Inspiration4, launched in 2021 and spent three days in orbit around the Earth.

The Apollo 17 mission, in 1972, was the last time humans walked on the moon.

Spacecraft must be designed to withstand extreme temperatures, from the intense heat of the sun to the freezing cold of deep space.

The Kuiper Belt is a region beyond Neptune that contains many small, icy objects, including dwarf planets like Pluto.

NASA's James Webb Space Telescope, set to launch in 2021, will be the largest and most powerful space telescope ever built.

In 2021, the United Arab Emirates became the first Arab country to send a spacecraft to Mars, called the Hope Probe.

Space exploration helps us learn more about the universe and our place in it, as well as inspire future generations of scientists and engineers.

The first spacecraft to orbit Mercury was NASA's MESSENGER, which arrived at the planet in 2011 and operated until 2015.

The International Space Station (ISS) is a space station that orbits around 250 miles above Earth.

It is the largest human-made object in space, measuring roughly the size of a football field.

The ISS is a joint project between five space agencies: NASA (USA), Roscosmos (Russia), JAXA (Japan), ESA (Europe), and CSA (Canada).

The first part of the ISS was launched into space in 1998, and the station has been continuously inhabited by astronauts since 2000.

The ISS is made up of multiple modules, including living quarters, laboratories, and observation windows.

Astronauts on the ISS conduct experiments in fields such as biology, physics, and astronomy to learn more about the effects of microgravity on the human body and other materials.

The ISS orbits the Earth once every 90 minutes, which means the astronauts on board see 16 sunrises and sunsets every day.

The ISS travels at a speed of around 17,500 miles per hour.

Astronauts on the ISS have to exercise regularly to prevent their muscles and bones from weakening in the microgravity environment.

The ISS has a recycling system that turns urine into drinking water.

The ISS is an international symbol of cooperation and peaceful collaboration among nations.

As of 2023, the ISS is expected to remain in operation until at least 2028, with plans to potentially extend its life even further.

The ISS is the third brightest object in the night sky after the moon and Venus, and can often be seen with the naked eye from Earth.

The ISS has a team of flight controllers on the ground who monitor the station 24/7 and communicate with the astronauts on board.

The ISS is equipped with a robotic arm called Canadarm2, which is used to capture and dock with visiting spacecraft.

Over 240 people from 19 countries have visited the ISS since it was first launched.

The ISS is protected from space debris and micrometeoroids by an outer layer of protective shielding.

Astronauts on the ISS use special toilets that use air flow to dispose of waste.

The ISS has a special "cupola" module with windows that provide a 360-degree view of Earth and space.

The ISS has hosted a number of high-profile visitors, including a Lego minifigure of "Star Wars" character Luke Skywalker and a guitar played by astronaut Chris Hadfield in a famous video performance of David Bowie's "Space Oddity."

The first rocket to reach space was the German V-2 rocket in 1944.

The Saturn V rocket, used by NASA during the Apollo program, is still the most powerful rocket ever built.

The first American to orbit the Earth was John Glenn, who did so in 1962 aboard the Friendship 7 spacecraft.

The first woman to go to space was Soviet cosmonaut Valentina Tereshkova in 1963.

The first American woman to go to space was Sally Ride in 1983.

The first privately funded spacecraft to reach space was SpaceShipOne, which flew to an altitude of over 100 kilometers in 2004.

NASA's Space Shuttle program, which ran from 1981 to 2011, consisted of five spacecraft that were designed to be reusable.

The Hubble Space Telescope, which was launched in 1990, has captured some of the most stunning images of the universe ever taken.

The International Space Station (ISS) is the largest and most complex spacecraft ever built, and has been continuously occupied since November 2000.

The first crewed mission to the Moon was Apollo 8 in 1968, which orbited around the Moon without landing on its surface.

The first humans to walk on the Moon were Neil Armstrong and Edwin "Buzz" Aldrin, who did so during the Apollo 11 mission in 1969.

The first space tourist was Dennis Tito, who paid $20 million to visit the ISS in 2001.

The first privately funded mission to the ISS was the SpaceX Dragon spacecraft, which docked with the station in 2012.

The Falcon Heavy rocket, developed by SpaceX, is currently the most powerful operational rocket in the world.

The Soviet Union's Sputnik 1, launched in 1957, was the first artificial satellite to orbit the Earth.

The first U.S. satellite, Explorer 1, was launched in 1958.

The Mercury program, which ran from 1958 to 1963, was the first human spaceflight program by the United States.

The Gemini program, which ran from 1961 to 1966, was the second human spaceflight program by the United States.

The Apollo program, which ran from 1969 to 1972, was the third human spaceflight program by the United States, and included the first missions to land on the Moon.

The Soviet Union's Buran spacecraft, which resembled NASA's Space Shuttle, flew only once, in 1988.

The Chinese space program sent its first astronaut into space in 2003, becoming the third country to independently send humans into space.

The Indian Space Research Organization successfully sent a spacecraft to Mars in 2014, becoming the first Asian country to do so.

The European Space Agency's Rosetta spacecraft made history in 2014 by landing a probe on a comet for the first time.

NASA's Voyager 1 spacecraft, launched in 1977, is currently the farthest man-made object from Earth and has entered interstellar space.

In the future, spaceships and rockets will play an important role in space tourism, asteroid mining, and the exploration of other planets and moons in our solar system.

The first rocket was invented by a Chinese inventor named Wan Hu in the 16th century.

The first liquid-fueled rocket was invented by American scientist Robert Goddard in 1926.

The first rocket to reach the Moon was the Soviet Union's Luna 2 in 1959.

The fastest rocket ever launched is NASA's Parker Solar Probe, which can travel at speeds of up to 430,000 miles per hour.

The Space Launch System (SLS) rocket, currently under development by NASA, will be the most powerful rocket ever built when completed.

The rocket engines on the Space Shuttle and the Saturn V were fueled by a combination of liquid oxygen and liquid hydrogen.

The first rocket launched from a plane was the Pegasus rocket, which is still used today.

The United Launch Alliance's Atlas V rocket is used to launch many of NASA's scientific spacecraft, including the Mars rovers.

The Soviet Union's Energia rocket was capable of carrying payloads of up to 220,000 pounds into orbit.

The Soviet Union's N1 rocket was designed to send cosmonauts to the Moon, but it never successfully completed a mission.

The Space Shuttle was the first spacecraft that could land on a runway like an airplane.

SpaceX's Crew Dragon spacecraft is the first crewed spacecraft to be launched from the United States since the Space Shuttle was retired in 2011.

The Soviet Union's Mir space station was the largest artificial satellite ever built until it was deorbited in 2001.

The Soviet Union's Venera 7 was the first spacecraft to successfully land on another planet, Venus, in 1970.

The Soviet Union's Mars 3 was the first spacecraft to successfully land on Mars in 1971.

The New Horizons spacecraft, launched by NASA in 2006, is the fastest spacecraft ever launched from Earth, reaching speeds of up to 36,000 miles per hour.

The Delta IV Heavy rocket, used by United Launch Alliance, is currently the second most powerful rocket in the world.

The Soviet Union's Salyut 1 was the first space station ever launched into orbit in 1971.

The Skylab space station, launched by NASA in 1973, was the first American space station.

The Chinese space program is currently developing a space station, which is expected to be completed by 2022.

The Russian Soyuz spacecraft has been used to transport cosmonauts to and from the ISS since 2000.

The Virgin Galactic SpaceShipTwo spacecraft is designed to take tourists to the edge of space for a brief suborbital experience.

Blue Origin's New Shepard spacecraft, named after astronaut Alan Shepard, is designed to take tourists to the edge of space for a brief suborbital experience.

The United Arab Emirates' Hope spacecraft successfully entered orbit around Mars in 2021, making it the fifth country to do so.

The future of space travel and exploration includes new rockets, reusable spacecraft, and even plans to send humans to Mars in the next decade.

The European Space Agency's Rosetta spacecraft successfully landed on a comet in 2014, becoming the first spacecraft to do so.

The Indian Space Research Organization (ISRO) sent a spacecraft to Mars in 2014 that cost less than the budget of the movie "Gravity."

In 2019, China became the first country to successfully land a rover on the far side of the moon.

The Canadian Space Agency's robotic arm, Canadarm, was used on numerous NASA space shuttle missions to deploy and repair satellites.

Japan's space program sent a spacecraft called Hayabusa to collect samples from an asteroid and return them to Earth in 2010.

France's space agency, CNES, developed the Ariane rocket, which is used to launch satellites into space.

In 2021, the United Arab Emirates' space program sent its first Mars mission, the Hope probe, to study the planet's atmosphere.

South Korea's space program has developed satellites to monitor environmental and weather patterns.

Brazil's space program has launched several satellites for Earth observation and telecommunications.

The Soviet Union, now known as Russia, was the first country to launch a satellite, Sputnik 1, into space in 1957.

The United Kingdom's space program has developed satellites for Earth observation and communications, and is involved in international space missions.

Israel's space program has developed satellites for Earth observation, communication, and defense.

Germany's space agency, DLR, has developed a number of scientific instruments and experiments for international space missions.

Australia's space program has developed satellites for Earth observation and telecommunications, and is involved in international space missions.

The United States' space program, NASA, has sent humans to the moon and developed numerous spacecraft for exploring our solar system.

Iran has launched several satellites for telecommunications and Earth observation.

Spain's space program has developed scientific instruments for international space missions.

Italy's space program has sent several missions to study asteroids, including the Hayabusa2 mission in collaboration with Japan's space agency.

Canada's space program has developed robotic technology for space exploration and scientific research.

The Netherlands' space program has developed technology for scientific research and satellite communications.

India's space program has a mission called Chandrayaan-2 that landed on the moon's south pole region in 2019.

Japan's space program launched the Hayabusa2 mission that successfully collected samples from an asteroid named Ryugu and returned to Earth.

Brazil's space program has launched several satellites to monitor the Amazon rainforest and study climate change.

Denmark's space program has a mission called ASIM that studies the effects of thunderstorms on the Earth's atmosphere and climate.

Portugal's space program has a mission called Infante that provides services for maritime surveillance, oil exploration, and disaster management.

The Austrian Space Forum (OeWF) conducts simulated Mars missions in the Moroccan desert to prepare for future manned missions to the red planet.

Norway's space program has a satellite named NorSat-1 that monitors maritime traffic, oil spills, and the Earth's environment.

Israel's space program has a privately-funded mission called Beresheet that attempted to land on the moon in 2019.

The Swedish National Space Agency (SNSA) has a satellite named Odin that studies the Earth's atmosphere and the cosmos.

SpaceX has developed reusable rockets that can be used for multiple launches, which has greatly reduced the cost of space travel.

In 2018, SpaceX launched the Falcon Heavy rocket, which is currently the most powerful rocket in operation.

SpaceX is planning to send a crewed mission around the Moon using the Starship spacecraft in the near future.

SpaceX has developed a system of landing legs that allow its rockets to land upright after launch, which helps save money and resources.

SpaceX's Starlink satellite network is expected to provide high-speed internet access to even the most remote areas of the world.

Amazon founder Jeff Bezos' Blue Origin is developing a rocket called New Glenn, which will be capable of launching payloads into orbit.

Bezos has invested over $1 billion of his own money into Blue Origin, demonstrating his commitment to space travel and exploration.

In addition to Blue Origin, Bezos has also invested in other space-related ventures, including the asteroid mining company Planetary Resources.

Billionaire Richard Branson's Virgin Galactic has already sold over 600 tickets for suborbital spaceflights, with prices ranging from $200,000 to $250,000 per seat.

Virgin Galactic's VSS Unity spacecraft can carry up to six passengers and two pilots.

ASTRONOMERS & ASTRONOMY

Johannes Kepler discovered that the planets move in elliptical orbits around the sun.

Tycho Brahe was a Danish astronomer who lost his nose in a duel and had a prosthetic made of gold and silver.

Caroline Herschel was the first woman to discover a comet.

Nicolaus Copernicus proposed the theory that the sun is the center of the solar system, not the Earth.

Edwin Hubble discovered that the universe is expanding, which led to the development of the Big Bang Theory.

Christiaan Huygens discovered the rings of Saturn and was the first person to suggest that Saturn has moons.

Annie Jump Cannon developed a classification system for stars that is still used today.

William Herschel discovered Uranus and several moons of Saturn.

Vera Rubin provided evidence for the existence of dark matter, a mysterious substance that makes up a significant portion of the universe.

Johannes Hevelius was a Polish astronomer who built his own observatory and was known for his detailed maps of the moon.

Henrietta Swan Leavitt discovered the relationship between the period and brightness of Cepheid variable stars, which allowed astronomers to determine the distances to faraway galaxies.

Anders Celsius, a Swedish astronomer, created the Celsius temperature scale that is used in most countries around the world.

Annie Jump Cannon was one of several women known as the "Harvard Computers" who analyzed astronomical data at Harvard University.

Hipparchus was an ancient Greek astronomer who made some of the earliest measurements of the positions and distances of stars.

Margaret Burbidge was a pioneering astrophysicist who discovered the presence of heavy elements in stars.

Edmond Halley accurately predicted the return of a comet that now bears his name.

George Ellery Hale founded the Yerkes Observatory and helped design the Mount Wilson Observatory, which housed the largest telescope in the world for many years.

Carl Sagan was a popular science communicator and astronomer who helped popularize astronomy with his book "Cosmos" and the television series of the same name.

Astronomers study objects in space, including planets, stars, galaxies, and black holes.

The study of astronomy dates back thousands of years, with ancient cultures such as the Egyptians, Greeks, and Maya all making important observations of the night sky.

The study of astronomy has led to many important technological advancements, such as GPS navigation and weather forecasting.

Astronomers have discovered an object in the outer solar system nicknamed "Farout," which is the most distant object ever observed within our solar system.

The discovery of "rogue" planets, which are not bound to any star and drift through space on their own, has expanded our understanding of planetary systems.

The discovery of the Kuiper Belt, a region of the solar system beyond Neptune that contains icy objects, has provided clues about the formation of the solar system.

Astronomers have discovered a galaxy that appears to be composed entirely of dark matter, with no visible stars or gas.

Astronomers have observed stars exploding in supernovas, which can be thousands of times brighter than the entire galaxy in which they reside.

The discovery of dark matter, a mysterious substance that makes up a large portion of the universe, has changed our understanding of the universe's structure and evolution.

The discovery of exoplanets with atmospheres that contain water vapor, methane, and other molecules has raised the possibility of finding life beyond Earth.

Astronomers have discovered a planet made of diamond, known as 55 Cancri e, that is eight times the mass of Earth.

The discovery of "megastructures" around a star, known as Tabby's Star, has sparked speculation about the possibility of alien technology.

Astronomers have observed "red sprites" and "blue jets" in Earth's atmosphere, which are mysterious electrical discharges high above thunderstorms.

Astronomers have discovered a star that is moving so fast it is escaping the Milky Way galaxy, known as "The Great Escape."

The discovery of "quark stars," which are even denser than neutron stars, has expanded our understanding of the most extreme objects in the universe.

Astronomers have discovered a galaxy that is producing stars at an astonishing rate, known as GN-z11, which is the most distant galaxy ever observed.

The discovery of "brown dwarfs," objects that are too large to be planets but too small to be stars, has expanded our understanding of stellar evolution.

Astronomers have discovered a "pulsar planet" orbiting a pulsar, a rapidly spinning neutron star that emits intense radiation.

Astronomers have discovered "diamond rain" on planets made of carbon, where high pressures cause diamonds to form and fall from the sky.

Astronomers have discovered a "galactic cannibal," a galaxy that is absorbing other galaxies and growing in size.

Astronomers have discovered a "dark galaxy," a galaxy that emits no visible light and is made up mostly of dark matter.

The word "telescope" comes from the Greek words "tele" and "skopein," which mean "far" and "to see," respectively.

Telescopes use lenses or mirrors to gather and focus light, making objects appear larger and brighter than they actually are.

The first telescopes were invented in the early 1600s by Galileo Galilei and Hans Lippershey.

The first telescopes were not very powerful and could only magnify objects by a few times, while modern telescopes can magnify objects by thousands or even millions of times.

The first telescopes were made using a combination of glass lenses and wooden tubes, and were often quite fragile and delicate.

Early astronomers often had to build their own telescopes from scratch, as there were no commercial manufacturers at the time.

The first telescopes were not well understood by the general public, and some people believed that they were magical devices that could see through walls and read people's thoughts.

Some telescopes, such as the Solar and Heliospheric Observatory (SOHO), are designed to study the Sun and its effects on Earth's climate and environment.

The largest telescopes on Earth are located on high mountains or in remote deserts, where there is less atmospheric interference.

The Atacama Large Millimeter/submillimeter Array (ALMA) in Chile is a network of telescopes that can observe radio waves from space and study the formation of stars and galaxies.

In addition to optical telescopes that use visible light, there are also telescopes that use other parts of the electromagnetic spectrum, such as radio waves and X-rays.

Frank Drake developed the Drake Equation, which estimates the number of civilizations in the Milky Way galaxy capable of communicating with us.

Georges Lemaître proposed the idea of the Big Bang, which is now the prevailing theory of how the universe began.

Stephen Hawking was a theoretical physicist who made groundbreaking contributions to our understanding of black holes and the universe.

Annie Jump Cannon was awarded the Henry Draper Medal, the first woman to receive this prestigious astronomy award.

Clyde Tombaugh discovered Pluto, which was later reclassified as a dwarf planet.

Neil deGrasse Tyson is a popular astrophysicist and science communicator who has hosted several television series on space and science.

Henrietta Swan Leavitt was deaf for much of her life, but she used her talents in astronomy to make groundbreaking discoveries about the universe.

Caroline Herschel was awarded a gold medal by the Royal Astronomical Society for her contributions to astronomy.

Johannes Kepler was a devout Christian who believed that the universe was a reflection of God's order and harmony.

Edwin Hubble was also a skilled athlete, and he played basketball and football in college.

Nicolaus Copernicus was a polymath who also worked as a lawyer, physician, and translator.

Tycho Brahe had a pet elk that he allowed to drink beer and died after falling down a staircase.

William Herschel was a talented musician and composer who wrote 24 symphonies in addition to his work as an astronomer.

Annie Jump Cannon was a suffragist who worked to secure voting rights for women in the United States.

Galileo Galilei was put on trial by the Catholic Church for his belief that the Earth revolves around the sun, which was considered heretical at the time.

Vera Rubin was not allowed to study astronomy as an undergraduate at Vassar College because she was a woman, but she went on to make groundbreaking discoveries in the field.

Johannes Hevelius built a wind vane on top of his observatory to track the direction and speed of the wind, which he believed could affect his observations of the stars.

Henrietta Swan Leavitt died of cancer at the age of 53, but her work continues to inspire astronomers today.

Stephen Hawking was diagnosed with ALS at the age of 21, but he continued to work and make important contributions to science throughout his life.

Despite our fascination with the possibility of extraterrestrial life, we have yet to find definitive proof that it exists.

Some scientists think that the conditions on Jupiter's moon Europa might be suitable for life. The moon has a subsurface ocean that could potentially support microbial organisms.

In 1977, a group of scientists sent a message into space in the hopes of contacting intelligent life. The message, which was sent to a cluster of stars 25,000 light years away, included information about our planet and human biology.

Some researchers suggest that extraterrestrial life may exist in the form of microscopic organisms that live in extreme environments, such as deep sea vents on other planets.

Strangely, a handful of scientists think that octopuses might actually be aliens that came to Earth through a process called panspermia, which is the idea that life can be distributed throughout the universe, from planet to planet.

The Hubble Telescope has been in space for over 30 years, but it's still going strong!

The Hubble Telescope is about the size of a school bus, but it only weighs about as much as two adult elephants.

The Hubble Telescope was launched into space on April 24, 1990, aboard the space shuttle Discovery.

The Hubble Telescope's orbit takes it around the Earth about once every 97 minutes.

The Hubble Telescope's camera can capture images with a resolution of 0.05 arcseconds, which is like being able to see a dime from 350 miles (560 kilometers) away!

The Hubble Telescope has been repaired and upgraded by astronauts on several occasions, which has allowed it to continue operating for more than 30 years.

The Keck Observatory is located on the summit of Mauna Kea, a dormant volcano in Hawaii.

The Keck Observatory's telescopes have a total light-gathering area of 70 square meters, which is equivalent to about 10 basketball courts.

The Keck Observatory's telescopes use a technique called interferometry, which combines light from multiple telescopes to create a more detailed image.

The Keck Observatory's telescopes have a dome that is 85 feet in diameter and weighs 300 tons.

The primary mirrors of the Keck I and Keck II telescopes are made of a special type of glass called Zerodur, which is more stable than traditional telescope mirrors.

The James Webb telescope is so powerful that it can detect a bumblebee on the moon!

The James Webb telescope will orbit the sun at a distance of 1.5 million kilometers from Earth, which is four times farther away than the moon.

The James Webb telescope has a special instrument called the NIRSpec, which can split light into its individual colors to reveal more about distant objects.

The James Webb telescope's mirrors are made of a special material called beryllium, which is strong and lightweight.

The James Webb telescope's sunshield is the size of a tennis court, and it's made up of five layers to protect the delicate instruments.

The James Webb telescope's gold-coated mirrors are specially designed to reflect infrared light, which is invisible to the human eye.

The James Webb telescope is one of the most expensive scientific instruments ever built, with a price tag of over $10 billion.

The James Webb telescope is so big that if it were a car, it would be longer than a school bus!

The James Webb telescope's primary mirror is made up of 18 hexagonal segments that will unfold once the telescope is in space.

The James Webb telescope's cameras are so powerful that they could read the text on a book from 2,000 miles away!

BLACK HOLES & GRAVITY

Black holes are incredibly dense objects with a gravitational pull so strong that nothing, not even light, can escape it.

The center of a black hole, where its gravitational pull is strongest, is called the singularity.

The event horizon is the point of no return around a black hole, where the gravitational pull is so strong that anything that crosses it is inevitably pulled into the black hole.

Black holes can form when a massive star runs out of fuel and collapses in on itself, or when two neutron stars merge.

The largest known black hole, called TON 618, has a mass of 66 billion times that of the sun.

Black holes can distort the space around them, causing time to slow down and even creating a phenomenon called gravitational lensing, where light from distant objects is bent around the black hole.

It's currently impossible to see a black hole directly, but scientists can detect them by observing the effects of their gravity on nearby objects.

The first image of a black hole was captured in 2019 by the Event Horizon Telescope collaboration, which used a network of telescopes around the world to create a virtual telescope the size of the Earth.

Black holes can spin, and the rate of spin can affect the size and shape of the event horizon.

Some black holes emit jets of high-energy particles from their poles, which can be detected by telescopes on Earth.

Black holes can merge together, creating even larger black holes.

The merging of two black holes can create ripples in the fabric of space-time, called gravitational waves, which were first detected in 2015 by the Laser Interferometer Gravitational-Wave Observatory (LIGO).

A black hole's gravity can also affect the orbits of stars around it, causing them to move in unusual ways.

If you were to fall into a black hole, you would experience a process called spaghettification, where the tidal forces of the black hole stretch you into a long, thin shape like spaghetti.

Black holes are not eternal, as they slowly evaporate over time through a process called Hawking radiation.

The first black hole was discovered in 1964 by astronomers Arno Penzias and Robert Wilson, who were studying the cosmic microwave background radiation.

The term "black hole" was coined by physicist John Wheeler in 1967.

The region around a black hole where the gravitational pull is so strong that it affects the motion of nearby objects is called the ergosphere.

Black holes can also be studied through simulations using supercomputers, which can help scientists understand their behavior and properties.

Some theories suggest that there could be "primordial" black holes that formed in the early universe, before the formation of stars and galaxies.

Some black holes are "quiet" and don't emit much radiation, while others are "active" and emit high levels of radiation, such as quasars.

Black holes can also have "accretion disks" of matter swirling around them, which can create intense heat and radiation.

Black holes can be billions of years old, and some of the supermassive black holes at the centers of galaxies may have formed less than a billion years after the Big Bang.

In theory, it's possible to create a black hole in a laboratory, but it would require an enormous amount of energy.

The gravity near a black hole is so strong that it can cause time to slow down, and even stop completely at the event horizon.

Black holes can also be "charged" and have an electric field, which can affect how they interact with other objects.

Black holes can create powerful cosmic explosions called gamma-ray bursts, which are some of the brightest and most energetic events in the universe.

Astronomers have discovered a supermassive black hole at the center of our own galaxy, which is thought to be 4 million times the mass of the sun.

Astronomers have observed "black hole burps," in which black holes release huge amounts of energy as they consume matter.

Astronomers have discovered a "cold quasar," a black hole that is surrounded by a giant reservoir of cold gas instead of the hot gas usually associated with black holes.

The Milky Way is our home galaxy, and it is made up of billions of stars, including our own Sun.

The Milky Way is a barred spiral galaxy, which means that it has a central bar-shaped structure and spiral arms that extend out from it.

The Milky Way is about 100,000 light-years across, which means that it would take 100,000 years to travel from one side to the other at the speed of light.

The Milky Way is estimated to contain between 100 billion and 400 billion stars, although the exact number is unknown.

The Milky Way is not static, and it is constantly rotating and moving through space.

The center of the Milky Way is called the galactic center, and it is located about 26,000 light-years from Earth.

The Milky Way's galactic center contains a supermassive black hole, which is about 4 million times more massive than the Sun.

The Milky Way is surrounded by a halo of dark matter, which is a mysterious substance that scientists can't directly observe but can detect through its gravitational effects.

The Milky Way's spiral arms are made up of gas, dust, and stars, and they contain regions of active star formation.

The Milky Way is home to many interesting objects, including nebulae, star clusters, and pulsars.

The moon has a very thin layer of dust on its surface.

The moon's phases are caused by the position of the moon in relation to the sun and Earth.

The moon's dark areas are called maria, which means "seas" in Latin.

The moon's light areas are called highlands or terrae.

The moon is covered in a layer of soil called regolith.

Scientists believe there may be more than 100 billion planets in our galaxy alone that could support life.

Some scientists believe that life on Earth may have been brought here by comets or meteorites from other planets or even other star systems.

The SETI Institute is an organization dedicated to the search for intelligent extraterrestrial life.

The famous "Wow!" signal detected in 1977 was a possible sign of extraterrestrial communication.

Some scientists believe that Mars may have once supported life, and that there may still be microbial life on the planet.

Printed in Great Britain
by Amazon